THE DUST OF THE WORLD

Also by Anthony Thwaite

Poems
Home Truths
The Owl in the Tree
The Stones of Emptiness
Penguin Modern Poets 18 (with A. Alvarez and Roy Fuller)
Inscriptions
New Confessions
A Portion for Foxes
Victorian Voices
Poems 1953–1983
Letter from Tokyo
Poems 1953–1988

Criticism
Contemporary English Poetry: an Introduction
Twentieth-Century English Poetry
Six Centuries of Verse
Poetry Today: 1960–1984

For Children
Beyond the Inhabited World: Roman Britain

Travel and Topography
Japan (with Roloff Beny)
The Deserts of Hesperides: An Experience of Libya
In Italy (with Roloff Beny and Peter Porter)
Odyssey: Mirror of the Mediterranean (with Roloff Beny)

As Editor
Penguin Book of Japanese Verse (with Geoffrey Bownas)
The English Poets (with Peter Porter)
Larkin at Sixty
Philip Larkin: Collected Poems
Selected Letters of Philip Larkin
Selected Poems of Longfellow

THE DUST OF THE WORLD

Anthony Thwaite

SINCLAIR-STEVENSON

First published in Great Britain in 1994
by Sinclair-Stevenson
an imprint of Reed Consumer Books Ltd
Michelin House, 81 Fulham Road, London SW3 6RB
and Auckland, Melbourne, Singapore and Toronto

Reprinted 1994

ISBN 1 85619 387 X

A CIP catalogue record for this book
is available from the British Library

Typeset by Deltatype Ltd, Ellesmere Port, Cheshire
Printed and bound in Great Britain by
Cox & Wyman Ltd, Reading, Berks

Notes and Acknowledgements

Several poems were first used by the following, and I am grateful to the editors and producers: *Bombay Literary Review*, BBC Radio 3, BBC World Service, *Critical Quarterly*, *Encounter*, *Literature Matters* (British Council), *London Magazine*, *London Review of Books*, *New Statesman*, *New Writing 1* (British Council), *Over the Bridge* (Puffin Books), *Poetry Book Society Supplement 1990*, *P.N. Review*, *Poetry Review*, *The Rialto*, *Spectator*, *A Garland for Stephen Spender*, *Sunday Times*, *The Times*, *Times Literary Supplement*.

The first seventeen poems in this collection were written during, or soon after, a stay in Japan, benefiting from a grant given me in October–December 1989 through the kindness of Shusaku Endo and Kenzo Kogi, and I am very grateful to them.

Several poems towards the end of the book were written in January–April 1992 during a semester as Poet-in-Residence at Vanderbilt University, Nashville, Tennessee, and I am grateful to that university for this appointment.

I have resurrected 'At Jamestown', written in 1970, included in my book *Inscriptions* (1973) but not included in any later collected volume, and have placed it in a new context among other 'American' poems.

I have also resurrected 'At the International Poetry Festival', published in the *New Statesman* in 1981 but never included in a book: written after an event in what was then Yugoslavia, it now reads with another kind of irony from what I may at the time have intended.

The poem now called 'Sarajevo: I' was written in 1973 and collected in my book *A Portion for Foxes* (1977), but not subsequently reprinted.

For Ann – together, apart

Contents

Cockroach Story

'The reason for a cockroach in a story must differ from the reason for a cockroach in a kitchen.'

Leon Wieseltier, *TLS*

It was not home. It was in Tokyo
At half-past ten at night or thereabouts.
I went into the kitchen, flicked the switch,
And saw him crouching on the table's edge.

He was enormous, brown, and very still.
His feathery branches waited, so it seemed,
For further movement, and for me to move.
We looked at one another very hard.

He did not move, nor did I, watching him.
The jet-lag left me drowsy still, though sleep
Seemed far away, as I was far away.
I studied him as if in Japanese.

Aburamushi is the name for him
I suddenly remembered, wondering
What *abura* means: *mushi* is 'insect' or
A dozen other things in Japanese,

Such as a kind of soup, both clear and poached.
This cockroach, though, was more a samurai,
Plated and helmeted and plumed and proud.
I faced him as a common yokel might,

Lest he should shove me sideways with his sword,
Or leap across the tabletop and land
Bristling with fury in my sweating hair.
It was a hot September night, and I

Was tired of travel. 'I'll get it over with –
This stinker from the floorboards makes me sick,'

I thought, 'and I am sick of fantasy.'
I took one slipper off and lunged at him.

He skidded off the table, hit the floor
With a soft slushy plop, and sidestepped back
Towards the sink. I threw myself full-length
And smashed him with the slipper, and crouched down.

His scales fanned out. He bled onto the boards,
Gave half a shrug, and then lay still and dead.
I wiped the slipper with a newspaper,
Rinsed both my hands, and groped my way to bed.

That is the story. This is the poem, told
In metre, with a rhyme to end it all.
The reasons for the cockroach, or the poem,
Or why I've told the story – who can tell?

A cockroach in a kitchen is the truth.
A cockroach in a story may be lies.
The insect was both noble and uncouth.
The writer makes a life from mysteries.

Butō

A stick; a stone; a shape with arms and legs.
The background, blank; the foreground, faces turned
Towards this stick, this stone, this shape – which then
Begins to move. Its robe is stained
(If it is called a robe). A man
Moves under it (if it is called a man).

And all so slowly, with such sense of pain:
The stick picked up, and then the stone, and both
Heavy as forests, heavy as boulders, each breath
Laboured, though silent. The robe, a rag
Torn between unseen hands. Again
The thing under it all reveals a man.

And this is art, for which you have to pay
To see a man bowed down by sticks and stones
And his own pain, against a wall which may
Be nothing but a rag, a trick
Along with all the pain and strain and stains
Enacted by a man, a stone, a stick.

The Last Byakkotai

I was the one who did not die.
Of course I died at last, but do not lie
With all the others, nineteen shafts of stone:
I, the one failure, lie alone
And nothing indicates the way I failed,
Evading suicide. My botched wounds trailed
Year after useless year, from youth to age,
While worshippers who come on pilgrimage
Remember my companions in their youth,
Eternal witnesses to blood and truth.

What was the glory that I did not earn?
This kind of truth is difficult to learn:
To reach sixteen, and fail, and spill your blood,
And so to be symbolic of some good
For which successive pilgrims will come far,
Light incense-sticks, and smell the smoke of war
Long vanished but still strong – or not succeed
And become infamous as one who tried to bleed
But did not bleed enough. No twentieth stone
Marks out the place I suffer in, alone.

Changes

After a day of cloud, a bright morning.
Sun prints a firm shadow on the screen.
Outside, green leaves are brilliant on a branch.

The abacus becomes a cash register
Reading the prices electronically.
Sony Walkmen walk the streets alone.

Cicadas, dying, slur their final notes
Before the evening crickets endlessly
Repeat their scales they say we cannot hear.

Night in the metropolis is a rainbow
Of distant neon, and my glaring lamp
Winks with a tremulous and silent shock.

Time is a moss, a river, and a stone.
Today grew cloudy as the Asian winds
Blew into the Pacific. Tomorrow lies

Pinned to the television screen's bright charts,
Clearer than weather, predicted in chirrupings
Spoken by girls who smile, and bow, and fade.

Shadows

Shadows at the door, through the door.
No one comes in. The television screen
Flickers news from Panama, ads for tampons.

Slurping of noodles, sucking of plenitude.
We eat alone, polite and separate:
Three Japanese, one foreigner. And then

The screen reveals a slaughtered chimpanzee
Which (if I understand the bulletin)
In Kyoto managed to pick up a key,

Unlocked his cage, and rampaged through the lab,
So had to be shot. We see his body, flat
Down in some other monkey's cage; we all

Look up from eels or noodles to take stock
Of something not like news, so singular
We look at one another in surprise

And murmur common nothings, and shake heads
In shared amazement that such things should be
Here in our little world of food and drink.

It doesn't last long. Apes are animals,
And we are human, though we're different,
Polite, and separate, beyond the shadows.

Festival

Autumn equinox: pink and white
The lanterns wave above the narrow street,
Swayed by a casual light September breeze.

Some lanterns lit, some dark: they'll soon come down,
After the families have visited
The shrines of all their dead, and brought their flowers,

And lit their sticks of incense, put to rights
The crowded little plots of earth and stone.
Look, they're already coming down: four men

Nimbly unstring them, take in loop by loop,
And concertina them to plattered disks,
Stack them in rows.

Much like the ordered dead
Under the lettered stones and staves and flowers,
The lanterns are put tidily away.

A whole year passes marked by rituals,
As if some punctuation must be here
To say what day or season has arrived

Again and yet again, in wind or rain,
Or simply by the calendar to prove
Things happened then, and now, and will again.

In Nara Park

The light goes in the deer park, and the deer are crying.
A young doe reaches for a lower branch
And plucks the paper prayer. Her soft lips munch
Somebody's wish for luck, or love. The leaves are dying,
Red, gold, and blackened on the shrine's dark path.

The old bucks cry and stumble, their moist breath
Poised in the cold air of this late afternoon.
The lanterns are unlit, and each white screen
Shows blind and still as a face set in death,
Fixed in its frame of carved and weathered stone.

The schoolchildren and tourists leave the park,
Letting these deer, these holy messengers,
Cry through the shadowy trees and gently browse
Where trees and lanterns merge into the dark,
Prayers hanging where the last light faintly shines.

Together, Apart

Too much together, or too much apart:
This is one problem of the human heart.

Thirty-five years of sharing day by day
With so much shared there is no need to say

So many things: we know instinctively
The common words of our proximity.

Not here, you're missed; now here, I need to get away,
To make some portion separate in the day.

And not belonging here, I feel content
When brooding on the portion that is spent.

Where everything is strange, and yet is known,
I sit under the trees and am alone,

Until there is an emptiness all round,
Missing your voice, the sweet habitual sound

Of our own language. I walk back to our room
Through the great park's descending evening gloom,

And find you there, after these hours apart,
Not having solved this question of the heart.

Terminal Happiness

To be conspicuous for complexion,
Length of nose, texture of hair,
Colour of eyes, cut of clothes,
Growth of facial stubble,
And posture of displacement.

To wait on Platform Zero
For a destination on the board
Indicated in characters
Capable of two readings
And in opposite directions.

To spend the blank interval
Rehearsing the simple numerals,
Copying the place-names,
Overhearing conversations
Punctuated with paranoia.

To board the train at last
Having checked with embarrassment
And for the third time
That it is indeed the right one
And not the non-stop express.

And finally to alight
At the station one intended
With no more luggage than necessary
And money for the next journey
On a bright October morning.

Sado

I

In the old port
between the lake and the sea,
a man plaiting fish-baskets,
fish-hawks crying,
hills soused in clouds.

Roofed trays of squid drying,
rain gathering in sheets
above collapsed huts.
Timelessly out-of-date,
a few faded words.

II

Jags of steep rocks, dragged cliffs
sifting down sand, crowned
with wind-spun pines, drowned
figurines in soft stone.

Villages straggling under
heaped maple hills, ridge-beams
heavy with hung persimmons
fronting the netted sea.

Bowed stunted women
pushing loaded carts
along narrow winding roads,
straws caught in the wind.

Above Ryotsu

Come here in the rain, under the dark pines,
Late afternoon in mid-November.
The steady rain drips from your umbrella.
No one visits the shrine above the little port.
It is not a famous place, this temple,
Unmentioned in the guidebooks. The stone lions
Grimace with ordinary rage, stare down
The avenue towards the new hotel.
Below, the ferry's foghorn blares twice, stops.

What strange needs made them build it here, and when,
Seems beyond explanation. Standing here
Under the rain, with nowhere to go
Except back to the hotel, is a banality
Equally inexplicable. This holiday
Comes at the wrong end of the year, away
From all the urgencies you've vanished from,
But satisfies another need, somehow:
To be foreign, tied to nothing, and yet happy.

No one will watch you, alone here in the rain:
Even the straggling schoolboys, going home,
Won't notice you, another dark dim shape
Beyond the torii, hidden in the mist.
Tomorrow you will take the ferry back,
Leaving the little port, the new hotel,
The temple with its lions, the wet pines;
And no one will have noticed anything,
Even your absence unremarked, at peace.

In the Missionary's House

After the persecutions and apostasies,
The tortures, crucifixions, secrecies,
The foreign fathers landed here again:
Two and a half centuries, and then
Came back to preach, to teach, and so to build.

And built this house. It is not an old house,
But even here, where few houses are old,
There are sounds: strains of something, not
Just earth tremors, come suddenly
At moments you don't expect –

Abrupt small punctuations, the dark wood
In beams and posts and floorboards snapping out
Orders or reactions, sometimes like a drum,
Sometimes a cry. In the missionary's house
They are like the sounds of something driven down,

Something suppressed, in pain, or leaping up
In joy to be back again, or murmurings,
Or prayers, or chants transformed to fossil wood
Yet capable of such articulation,
Such firm insistence in this foreign place,

Night in the missionary's house can be
A deep uneasiness at what has happened
Between the ceaseless crickets, and the drums
Come from the far temple, and the hush
Of wind and rain against the insect screens:

Until the dawn, when the birds start again,
Cicadas chatter in a different key,
The trucks and cars hurry familiarly,
And the missionary's house stands square and clear
In its old place, though not so very old.

Potter

He took a lump of clay,
Squatted above his wheel,
Threw it a certain way,
Spun it till you could feel
His thumbs splay out the rim
And spin and spin and spin,
Then pulled, and pressed, and let
The clay become a jet
Rising, controlled by air,
Then let it go; and there,
Below the plume of clay,
Cut it and made it stay
Perfect, a moulded bowl.
Three more grew from the whole
Pillar of clay, and lay –
Accomplishments, and final.
                                        Till he took
These four perfections like a finished book
And closed the pages with his open hands,
Collapsing clay back into clay. His smile
Mocked at the skill he nullified, while
Only the shapeless lump remains and stands.

After the Japanese

I

If only, when the news came through
Old Age was on the way,
One shut the door, said 'Not at home',
And turned the bore away.

II

Though I had always known it was the way
I had to follow at the very end,
I never thought as yesterday went by
That it would be the road I walk today.

Legend

The superstitious Japanese
Are an inevitable prey
To devils, goblins, sprites; and these
Can be invoked, they say.

So thought U.S. Intelligence,
With forces poised to invade Japan.
It made a certain sort of sense
To an American

Who, studying stories soaked in age,
Myths stretching back to fabled days,
Pondering legends page by page,
Found one which would amaze

The credulous little men who hid
In the last island on the way.
This ploy was an impressive bid
To bring the end of play.

Foxes, caught wild and dipped in bleach
And trapped in waiting landing-craft,
To swim ashore, where they would reach
The Japs . . . The experts laughed,

And saw, already, terrified
Soldiers throw down their limbs and arms.
The fox is almost deified
By Japanese, and charms

Are sold at shrines to ward them off –
And yet they're very holy too:
A mixture at which none could scoff –
Bad news, half-gods, and *true* . . .

The trouble was the sea, which bore
Most of the ghostly white away.
Some forty foxes swam ashore
And scampered round the bay.

These sodden creatures, scared and tamed
And stripped of all their ghostliness,
Looked humbled, miserable, ashamed,
Shrunk to a nothingness.

And then it was the Japanese
Who laughed, and sighed, and primed their guns.
Cultural errors such as these,
Indeed, are anyone's.

Interpreter

I am very nervous. You can tell I am very nervous.
The moment I greet you, I begin talking too much
And the words are not right, I know they are not right.
Anyway . . . They have asked me to do this job
Which means speaking your words in my words
And their words in your words, and so I begin
Talking too much before you have even begun
Using many words at all. In fact, as I say . . .
Anyway . . . I wish I could keep calm, and listen, and say
Exactly the words that they speak and you speak, and begin
To know what you want to know about what that is
Over there (I'm not sure – I think it historical).
Anyway . . . But now I begin to tell you about my life
Since you kindly asked a question, and so I go on –
Too much, too much – about father who passed away, and
        mother ill,
And how I was ill too, often, when young, and how
I never became married, because my fiancé
Disappeared – no, not exactly, he just stopped coming, and . . .
Anyway . . . That was a famous temple, I forget the name.
And I am a Latter Day Saint, which is very strange,
I know, in this country, but I know it is true for me,
And could be for you – but you are a Protestant,
Have I got the word right? And I have my faith, yes I do,
And though I am nervous I know it is true for me,
Though my colleagues despise me, and whisper about me, and
        are rude
In front of my face and behind my back, and I . . .
        Anyway . . .
Yes, I think we are stopping a moment to see this famous
Historical place, I forget the name, I don't know the words,
And believe me, believe me, believe me, dear foreign guest
(So kind in your questions, so gentle, so worried – I see)
You are welcome here, very welcome. Anyway . . .
Please excuse how nervous I am. I think I shall die.

Gairaigo*

Sitting in apāto
Quiet in my manshon
I write this in my nōto,
Lacking a wāpuro.

I am on a tsuā
From faraway Yōroppa
Where I wear a toppā
Or ōbā in the winter.

Terebi and rajio
Speak to me Nihon-go.
Tabako, arukōru
Help my arubaito.

Invite me to a konpa,
Give me a haibōru,
I have no abekku . . .
Show me please the toiré.

Better fetch shaberu.
Now I need a beddo,
Feeling pretty ierō . . .
Ga-gi-gu-ge-go.

*Japanese 'words that come from outside'

apartment; mansion (block of flats); notebook; word-processor; tour; Europe; topcoat; overcoat; television; radio; cigarettes; alcohol; work (from Ger. *arbeit*); party; highball; girl-/boyfriend (from Fr. *avec*); toilet; shovel; bed; yellow.

Alms

Two things the size of whittled pencil stubs
Poke through the taxi window, pink streaked black.
And through the window drifts a plaintive voice
Spun from a mouth that's also pink and black.

Leper, or thalidomide, or maimed –
What's diagnosed at this brief traffic halt?
My eyes averted from his eyes on me,
Why should I feel that this is all my fault?

Yet reach, of course, into my wallet thick
With crumpled little notes worth nothing much.
The accelerator roars. The pincered pencil stubs
Catch at the offering. We do not touch.

And all the distance to the airport, trapped
In a tight vacuum of sweat and dust,
That voice beseeches and those stubs implore.
Ignore this if you like. Or want. Or must.

Calcutta: 1830

We carried Bibles, Shakespeare, Bacon, Locke.
Temples and shrines storeyed with tangled limbs
Held things unwholesome. How to tend our flock
When Krishna cast out Matthew, and our hymns

Were drowned by prayers to Pooja? Addison
Might teach them a pure style but could not teach
Serious piety. To make comparison
Between our code and theirs was out of reach.

Untouchables in their fastidious way,
Yet sedulous in following the text:
They sat and read, but would not kneel to pray.
Something within them balked, and sulked, and vexed.

Here on the shelf, two images contend:
Francis, his face transfigured with God's love,
And Jagannath, whose eyes blaze and distend.
They stand together. But they do not move.

Our cemetery holds such images,
In Park Street, where we buried our own kind;
But who can hazard what our gardener sees,
Who, quietly chanting to himself, is blind?

Tughluqabad

These ruins did not need me to record them:
They told themselves of ruin as they rose
High on the banks that Tughluq built to hold them.
They told what he had built they would depose.

These tall slumped walls, these domes pocked deep with holes,
These slopes strewn hopelessly with shattered stone,
Were destined to be broken like the bowls
And jugs and pitchers smashed, sherds split with bone,

Their terracotta bleached white in the sun.
Only one emblem rises up and stirs
Life back into their death: vermilion,
Slashed deepest blue, a peacock screams and veers

Up from a brackish pool, its brilliant fan
Thrown out, then folded, volleys towards a tree.
The ruins crumble in the steady sun.
The peacock hides in swathes of greenery.

More Indian Images

The edicts of Ashoka cut in rock.
A rat behind the bar sniffs at a glass.
The langurs in the branches leap across
Festoons of foliage. The station clock
Is stuck at Queen Victoria's jubilee.

At Dhali in the rock-cut shrine I take
Honey and yoghurt from the offered hand.
At Puri the big waves break on the sand
Among the sewage. The village potters bake
Soft earthenware under a heap of gorse.

Mother Teresa's famous hospice stands
Against the compound plot where Shuju Roy
Recalls how things were when he was a boy.
His grandpa knew Tagore. With folded hands,
The sage in Oxford with a stiff-necked youth.

At Bhubaneshwar the majestic cart
Of Jagannath is hammered tier by tier.
The Lord's eyes blaze like fury at your fear.
This is the night halt. Next morning, you will start
Another journey, on another day.

The Rug

Among the red and yellow tangles
Grubs squirm, wings brush the rotten weavings,
The fabrications of a Basra market.

The old couple have not noticed. They sit
Among their trophies of Iraq and India,
Accumulations of five decades' journeys.

He was an envoy. Now he tells us how
He will write a book that proves the Maori
Voyaged from Libya, left inscriptions there.

She was a pianist, studied under Schnabel.
She thinks she remembers Schoenberg. Her legs swell,
Her tight white bandage stained with orange pus.

In the corner of their room, along a shelf,
Six Buddhas squat and praise longevity.
The rug from Basra crawls with bright decay.

Recreational Leave

They have come back. The next lot is in,
Landing at the port. Soon they will be here,
Some a little bit drunk, some a lot drunk,
With their money, their condoms, their loud pink faces.

They will be here soon. I tidy up the place,
Making the mattress nice, hanging the curtain
Just in the right place, bringing the water
So they can have a wash before it begins.

And afterwards too: they like to have a good wash
Before and after. I put out a tray with two cups,
Which some of them will fill with whisky or beer
And some of them will not. I want to make them happy.

Some of them are happy already, but I hope not too happy.
I don't want a lot of noise, or slapped faces,
With my baby here close by under the netting.
On a good night, I can have maybe ten of them in

With their money, their condoms, their loud pink faces,
And no trouble at all, if they are not too happy
With whisky or beer or whatever they want to do
To show they are proper men and enjoying themselves.

Nobody wants any trouble. Anyway, I don't.
If they are happy, and pay, and go away,
I shall be happy. My aunt will be happy too.
I put on my good dress, and wait for the sound

Of their funny voices banging about outside,
And try to guess what sort of a night it will be.
Baby, be quiet. I am happy. I am fifteen.
This is the way I live, on the edge of the port.

At the Struga Festival

for George Szirtes

'There stood a man of Macedonia, and prayed him, saying,
Come over into Macedonia, and help us.'

Acts, 16:9

The Hyatt Regency in the capital,
As big as Diocletian's palace, tranquil.
Tourists eschew the smell of civil war.

Then the plane south to Struga, and four score
Poets converge to celebrate the Word,
Speaking in tongues. One local well-oiled bard
Greets us with bloodshot eyes, then falls away.

A shower of fireworks; poems; speeches. Day
Breaks brilliant on the lake as rumours run
Hither and thither, polyglot and loose.
A seminar with headphones. Can you scan
Slavic hexameters? The tree of man
Was never quiet. How define the Use
Of Poetry when the referendum looms?

Brodsky the Laureate is absent. Tombs
Carved for dead kings surround the citadel.
Bulgars and Greeks among us mutely tell
Legends of empire. On the bridge, more verse.

The situation in the North grows worse.
The airport bus. Embraces. Flying home,
We see the placid lake busied with foam.

Elegy

No haven and no shelter and no home.
A language tangled among frontiers –
Quick rivers, mountain chains, sand barriers.
Come out of nowhere, nowhere can they come
Into a place that they can call their own.
Far to the south, mud ruins' syllables
Spill across deserts, potsherd-littered tells:
Ur, Eridu, Kish, faces of stone,
Eroded Babylon, abandoned gaols
Whose brick on brick the conquerors laid low
Among the dunes, so low, so long ago,
Where now the serpent gathers up its trails
Ready to strike at enemies to come.

No haven and no shelter and no home.

Freedom

Through the vast crowded wards, thousands came round.
Limbs twitched; mouths opened, uttering strange old cries;
Wild smiles and tears, and snarls at what went on
Through decades of paralysis.
                                        Bodies are found
Strewn in the corridors. A doctor lies
Battered in blood. The warders have all gone,
Savaged by patients who woke up to see
The doors were open. Healers are unmasked
As torturers; nurses crucified
When drugs, withdrawn, reveal them all to be
Captors and guards.
                                And those who this way died
Are faceless as their patients.
                                        And some asked
How the great hospital would care for those
Who lie there still, free, in a deep repose.

At the International Poetry Festival

for Douglas Dunn

I think I can recognise the word *freedom*
In seventeen languages. It seems to be popular.
Here is another poet at the microphone
Waving an arm here and an arm there.
And now an African who writes in English
Prays that the rivers will flow with torrents of blood,
And I want to talk to him about Enoch Powell.
But now an Italian takes over, mellifluous,
Telling us the festival means *pace* and *bella*
And of course *libertà*, and then there are several
Odes to the Leader, and the self-invited American
Prowls round the back of the stage muttering
Not in protest but because he needs a fix.
In the front row an Indian falls asleep.

One hundred and seventy-six poets are groaning with boredom
In the warm summer air as the moths interfere
With the television lights in the fragrant southern air.
The brows of the organisers are shining with sweat
And exhaustion and alcohol, but at least they know
One hundred and seventy-six poets, with subsidised travel
And supported by generous hospitality, have arrived –
Some of them famous outside their own countries,
Some notorious inside them as well.
It is good for the autonomous republic, it is good for the hotel
Where all these bards bed down after fourteen hours
Devoted to symposia, slivovitz, and hanging about in the lobby
Complaining about their hosts, their fellow-delegates, their
        digestion.
I do not know the Mongolian for *freedom*.

(1981)

Sarajevo: I

The name is history.
                              The thick Miljacka flows
Under its bridges through a canyon's breadth,
Fretted with minarets and plump with domes,
Cupped in its mountains, caught on a drawn breath.

There on the pavement, absurd souvenir
Of past dramatics, Princip's spoor is set:
The exact spot, the precise grid of war,
A kerbside view of a choked and bloody street

Where, regiments in step, a world moves
Or drifts away from its moorings like a ship
Propelled down-river between crowded wharfs
And only a collision can make it stop.

The muezzin calls, the bells and pigeons float
Above Sephardic, Muslim, Catholic graves:
Provincial, dated, their low stones map out
Haphazardly the place that history chose.

(1973)

Sarajevo: II

'Narrow streets, profane and sacral architecture'
Sarajevo: A Guide, Dr Smail Tihic, 1973

The sacred is profaned, profanity
Thumps its large casual lobs on narrow streets
Where people queue for bread, fill buckets, sprint
Through dereliction towards safety. See
How none are safe. See how each building greets
Each blurred escapist with a different hint
Of how each separate faith may end in grief,
And some in blood.

And twenty years ago I got it wrong –
Fit emblem for a past I never knew
But saw as ikon for a long-gone war.
It was an elegy, a plangent song
Composed out of composure: nothing new.
I saw the place, I struck a spark from flint.
There is nothing sacred, only profane belief:
Nothing understood.

(1993)

Final Verdict Tours

Having crossed the ultimate checkpoint to our friendly nation,
You have twenty minutes to see this ancient city.
There is the Black Fort and the Basalt Church,
The Basilica of Unrighteousness, the Mosque of Envy,
The Lukewarm Baths, and the successive quarters
Inhabited by the Extremish, the Waverish, the Vilipends.

Behold the monuments to antique unfortunates:
The sad exit of Hadad the Excitable
Torn to pieces in a popular rising,
The sublime martyrdom of Rashap the Vulgar
Subdued by applied arachnids under the armpits.
We are proud of our heritage among such enactments.

Observe our more recent manifestations of culture –
The picturesque garments of the tolerated minorities,
The gorgeous pictography of the eliminated tribes.
(Avoid the offered sherds, the reproductions:
You may be seduced by cunning artifices
Replicated in the bazaars and in humble courtyards.)

Here are the products of the curious contemporary,
Desirable to those with an eye for excellence:
Embroideries by hand, paintings by foot
Achieved by those whose hands have been excised
For various offences considered capital
But for the amnesty of our President and his mercies.

We allow for a rest-stop at the end of such plenitude –
A packed lunch available, the spirits extra:
Any currency is valid, though temptingly fluctuating.
Then back to the bus, please, in orderly fashion.
Tonight at Happy Hour the evening's rubric.
Tomorrow our departure for the last resort.

The Rev. C.L. Dodgson

Somewhere in Oxford, in a Christ Church quad
Or by the Cherwell's sluggish brownish flow,
You watch a nervous slender scholar go
Muttering to himself, perhaps, or God.

He talks to little girls who talk to flowers.
To them he does not stammer. His mild eyes
Gaze at what is, turn it contrariwise,
And penetrate a world that is not ours.

And yet it is our world, made happy-mad,
Where playing-cards and cats, chessmen and sheep,
Inhabit those asylums where we sleep
Beyond the logics that we thought we had:

Beyond sense, things at which to laugh or weep,
Where everyone is guilty, no one sad.

Accumulations

The exhaustion of museums, of libraries:
It is nothing to do with dust, or being old, or dead.
The dust is removed daily, and the ageing is also our own.
As for being dead, we can live with that.

No, it is the accumulation of so many pasts,
So many things written, things made, each so different
They cover the universe with their quiddities.
We grope hopelessly through all this stuff.

Each page, each book, each sherd, each pot, bequeaths us
A multitude of silted pasts. To read them,
To bring them back to life in whole or fragment,
Exhausts us. We look up, are blinded by them.

It will not stop. We step through endless doors
Opening and shutting, going on down avenues
And corridors, between cases and shelves, until
The doors close behind us. Even then, it will not stop.

For after that, the others follow us
And find us piecemeal in succeeding rooms,
In stacks of cabinets, ranged along drawers, in spools
Of tiny film that turns and turns and turns.

Levellings

Where people lived, where people threw their things,
Their piles of mess, their bonfires, secrets, scraps,
All end like this, these endless levellings,
Shaded and laid in contours, like old maps.

The damp mud cliff, laid open as a sore
Dripping its weight of yesterday made bare,
Unloads a cataract of petty lore
Which I pick over, delve into, and share.

From East and West these lived-with things once came,
I name them as I take them in my hand:
Some valued once, or ordinary, the same
Bits of a past I grope to understand.

And grope towards a meaning in our mess,
A sudden knowledge of this piece of past,
Whether of value or quite valueless,
Of what will fall away or what will last.

Gone

Down in the dark water
Where the quick mill-race flows,
Something hidden rises,
Something secret goes.

Rising, it flashes whitely.
Going, it sinks below.
You cannot recognise it.
You see the water flow

Quickly under the mill-race,
Race down and reach the pond.
Whatever you have seen there
Goes on and out, beyond

Your vision or your knowledge,
Untethered to one place.
It glints, and hints, and teases,
And shows you your own face

Peering below the sluice-gate,
Watching the mill-race fall
Forever and forever,
With not a word at all

Of what you saw – or fancied
You saw – rise up and sink
One moment in the water,
The next over the brink.

The Dust of the World

Proverbs, 8:26

Unseen until it settles, all around
It hovers in the crannies of itself,
So faint and soft it never makes a sound.
It gathers on the books along the shelf.

My finger strokes it from a pot-plant leaf.
The leaf would fall without it anyway.
The dumbness of the world, numbness of grief,
Settling on silence, well prepared to stay.

The world, the flesh, the devil – these old runes,
Renunciations of this trinity,
Themselves drift off, like half-forgotten tunes
Into the dustbowls of infinity.

Memoir

He writes what he remembers, innocent,
Though now he is no longer innocent:
What he remembers, what he tries to write,
Is how things were. He cannot get it right.

The words go down on paper. In between
Another sheet of paper lies between
The sheet he writes on and the page beneath.
Something is lying down there, underneath.

And it is those words, on the page below,
That somehow stick, as he goes down below
Experience to innocence, and finds
The thing he looked for is the thing he finds.

But in the morning, reading what he wrote
Last night, the only words he finds he wrote
Are on the surface. And the page below
Is blank as things he did not want to know.

Nescit vox missa reverti

The voice, or word, that goes
Far out into the world
Lies on the ear or page.
Water and metal flows,
Ice melts, steel weapons hurled
Towards another age.

What drops, and sticks, and stays
(These words that seem so frail)
Settles. It makes its stand.
Through brief and shifting days,
Fading, receding, pale,
It shows the living hand

That wrote them, transmits the voice
That spoke them. So we see
Years later what was said,
Written or spoken, choice
Not theirs to oversee,
Not theirs, who now are dead.

For George MacBeth

Wasted away –
Limbs, speech, and breath –
Such mockery, such sprightly gay
Spirits smothered, friend
Stubborn to call it death.
Make it all end.

Last words are right:
You whispered them
That last intolerable night,
Darkness itself, deep
Gathering of choked phlegm –
'How long will I sleep?'

The Notebooks

To turn again these faded pencilled pages,
Their neatly cancelled lines, precisely dated,
Their doodles of frustration, sudden rages
Or mocking self-contempt, before the next
Refining or reduction's contemplated,
And then the immaculate and final text –

This is to hear you speak, not just to read you,
Familiar words-by-heart plumbed deep and strange
Down to the nerve of hurt, the pains that feed you
Raw as they are, a present tense, not past,
Thronged with the power to strengthen through their change,
Poised to the lines we know, and built to last.

Elegy for George Barker

And there, beneath a bull-nosed Buick
Inert in Kensington, the poet lay,
Grease smeared on cheek-bones, a fallen god
Who rose to greet me, seventeen, with Blake
And Langland in the triptych. Stay
Yet a little longer, genius of the place,
Fitting my footprints in the prints you trod,
Letting me see those lineaments, that face.

It was apotheosis. It was epiphany.
Already there were elegies at hand,
Mellifluous and celebrating
The mystery that was also poetry.
Whatever words flew up, whatever scanned,
Became that moment. St George had claimed his own.
Imago, image, creator and creating
Took root within the reliquary bone.

Years past, years gone. I have learnt since then
You were no god, for only God is that.
That was a truth I know you would endorse.
And yet some angels mingle among men,
And have some essence, pure, dark, uncreate,
Extending through subtention. This was yours.
You rose, and fell, and took your vagrant course
Among men, mandrake, and all mysteries.

The vocative takes off in memory,
Almost becomes a perfect O to bless
Your wicked simulacrum resting there,
Elbow on bar, seducing those like me
From Id and Ego with your sophistries.
Forget it. What we never shall forget
Is that brow-wrinkled, basiliskian stare
Stabbing at the cold heart. It stabs me yet.

In Memory of Howard Nemerov

Convened, if not coerced, four years ago
At an all-chattering jamboree for rampant egos
In the silver dollar state of Colorado,
You stood like a pillar of some rarer metal
Muttering asides in a sort of heightened prose
Between your poems, of which each syllable
Distinctly stood as proof that sanity
Still had something to do with poetry.

The laughs from those who heard you mostly came
In the right places, and naturally you forbore
To point out to the thin audience that your name
Was unlikely to fill a theatre like this,
In spite of all the 'honours' that you wore.
Wry smiling wilful brilliant courtesies –
I see you now, as then, a self-styled dinosaur
Magnificent on the muddy, slipping shore.

September 3rd 1939: Bournemouth

My summer ends, and term begins next week.
Why am I here in Bournemouth, with my aunt
And 'Uncle Bill', who something tells me can't
Be really my uncle? People speak
In hushed, excited tones. Down on the beach
An aeroplane comes in low over the sea
And there's a scattering as people reach
For towels and picnic gear and books, and flee
Towards the esplanade. Back at the hotel
We hear what the Prime Minister has said.
'So it's begun.' 'Yes, it was bound to.' 'Well,
Give it till Christmas.' Later, tucked in bed,
I hear the safe sea roll and wipe away
The castles I had built in sand that day.

Evacuation: 1940

Liverpool docks. The big ship looms above
Dark sheds and quays, its haughty funnels bright
With paint and sunlight, as slim sailors shove
About with chains and hawsers. Mummy's hand
Is sticky in my own, but I'm all right,
Beginning an adventure. So I stand
On a deck piled high with prams, the staterooms shrill
With mothers' mutterings and clasped babies' cries.
I squirm and tug, ten years impatient, till
Loud hootings signal something . . . The surprise
Of hugging her, feeling her face all wet:
'Mummy, you're sweating.' They were tears; not mine.
She went away. I was alone, and fine.

Pleasure, and guilt. Things you do not forget.

Maturity: 1944

A son, fourteen, home to father and mother
After four years away. The one who went
A child, this one returning as a man
Almost: his voice broken, speaking American.
He was their son, but somehow now another:
The years of absence forced them to invent
New habits for this foreigner.
                                        So then
The father, fooling about, faced up to the boy,
Put up his fists: they could behave like men
In manly parody. And the son, to join in the game,
Put his up too, pretending they were the same,
And struck. The father's nose gushed out with blood.
The son watched, appalled. And never understood
Why his father leapt, and cried, and cried with joy.

Washington Again

That iron bridge, high above Rock Creek Park,
The embassies along the avenue,
The turn uphill among porches and dry trees –

I recognise them all as if today
Were not a full half-century ahead
Of when I knew them first. Now I go left

Down by Wisconsin; there in front of me
The school's big dusty playground where some boy
Told me horrific stories about sex.

Wartime. War has helmets, uniforms,
The Zero and the Spitfire crayon-traced,
Dutiful letters ('Mummy, Daddy') sent.

And then, close by, the red-brick library
In which I first read Ransome, Tarkington,
Rummaged among the reference books which gave

Details of Bolivian governments
And all the North American Indian tribes.
Small Georgetown streets, and swallowtails, and shops

I looked at then but never went inside,
And don't go now . . . What sick excitements lurch
Back to those days I see and recognise

But knew as little as today? A child
Lingers among the shadows in the heat.
I have been back, with nothing more to tell.

At Jamestown

By Greyhound south from Washington's white domes,
Passing low factories and supermarkets,
Along a road where no one ever walks
But touched only by hot and whining rubber,
I reach the first frail enclave of these states.

Jamestown. Its relics dredged from swamp and fever,
It lacks even the substances of ruins
But must be dug for in its lost encampments,
Each scrap and sherd and shred disjected tokens
Of failure never staunched, of pointless landfall.

Imperial peninsula! Beyond
The crammed museum the rich landscape swarms
With cemeteries of cars, the stench of waste
Fanned upward from Virginia's garbage cans,
The sewage of a whole half continent.

Magnolia comes to blossom as the cameras
Snap at these smaller, rarer sediments.
Down the brown estuary fresh water flows,
And far behind it all the prodigal
And violent issue briefly fathered here.

(1970)

The Mantis at Williamsburg

Hidden within a lattice of thin leaves,
You spend eternity brooding on a leaf
As green and ageless, as remote and brief
As ancient texts nobody now believes:
But when you move at last, you move like one
Who accurately gauges what's begun.

Miniature dinosaur, perfect, preserved,
Jointed with geology's delays
To prove the past is present, every day's
A new conviction that what we observed
In fossil jaw, eye, limb, is with us still,
Revolving in your hungry mandible.

Beyond your jungle lies the present time,
Preserved less perfectly, a kind of past
That adumbrates how things unwilled to last
Last in their quaintness only. From the slime
Out of whose swamps you came, your eyes reject
The preservationists' desired effect.

This neat museum is a decorous trick,
A trick of Time which, always somewhere else,
Measures the faltering and uncertain pulse,
The wavering move, or clutch, that cannot pick
Whatever prey flies in within our range.
We make pretences here. You do not change.

Old South

Old Dominion, Old Heritage, Olde Glory Fireworks,
Olde Discount, Old Hickory, Old Grandad, Old South.

How new it all is, vacant lots, gas stations, the WALK signs
flashing abruptly and whitely,
Dad's Old Bookstore crammed with Confederate lore,
a First of *I'll Take My Stand* priced far above rubies,
the Antique Malls, the Primitive Collectibles,
all among drive-ins and thruways
and sidewalks where I am the only walker,
eccentric among odd joggers, waiting for the WALK sign.

And suddenly, at this intersection, the slope
running one way downtown in this urban wilderness,
looking at that slope down to a battered frame building
(a house maybe, once, or a store gone derelict),
my eyes take in a distant simulacrum:
Don Abrahams' farm in Fairfax County, Virginia,
in the dip of the country road that ran from my uncle's house.

It was 1940. I was new from England.
Don and I played in his yard, and he took me to shake the
hand of
Pa Abrahams, 90, old grandad, skinny in his rocking chair,
and then to see
out back, on a peg, a small shabby grey peaked cap,
the little Confederate drummer-boy's, back in '64.

Old Mobile Estates, Grand Ole Opry, Old Hickory TV
Appliances,
Old Timer Log Homes Marketing, Old South.

Snakes (Virginia, 1940)

Down in the creek, snakes:
Snakes in the opposite wood.
There were snakes everywhere.
This was new. This was good.

At home in England, snakes
Were pets in a glass cage.
Here they slipped free, and swam.
This was a golden age.

Most folk I knew hated snakes,
Shrank if I brought one back
And let it run over my arm
Or gathered and then lay slack.

Whipsnakes, cornsnakes, snakes
Swollen, and black, and green,
Crept through my days and nights.
This was the primal scene.

And there were other snakes,
Ones to be cautious of:
Cottonmouths, copperheads, once
A rattler I saw in a grove.

How to account for these snakes
In a boy uprooted at ten
In a war that spanned a world
He would not see again?

Eden did not have snakes:
Only one snake, it is said.
We know what that single snake
Did. Or so we have read.

I had not read it then.
All I knew was I loved the things.
Years on, I call them all back,
Sinuous rememberings.

Sunday by Belmont

The ante-bellum, gracious, columned, white,
Holds itself back in this high mansion, dead
Sure of nothing but its being right,
Its 'sense of values' others have long shed.

Tradition, that gaunt fugitive civic ghost,
Erects its shrines, its annals, its steel plaques.
The few-starred flag defiantly is tossed
Above a shopping-mall where only blacks

And a few derelicts one might call white
Wait at the bus-stop: others hurtle off
Towards vague neighborhoods, in daily flight
Down highways hacked sheer, sharp, a limestone trough

Speeding the Gadarene across the state
But not over the cliff. At least, not yet.
Among the unfavoured stationed few I wait
Here at the bus-stop. Winter breezes fret

That antique flag over bleak carpark wastes,
Defeat, defiance souring, as I board:
Downtown to Christ Episcopal. My tongue tastes
The bitter wine of some unrisen Lord.

Franklin and Nashville: 1864

These tracks of blood over these frozen ruts
Were made by unshod men,
Hood's threadbare remnant. Watch them, then,
Stumble across the scrub, as from the heights
Others are watching: in those piled redoubts
Cannon and howitzers incline
And rake the ragged line.

Retreat and stand, fire and fall back. The trees,
Armoured with ice, are bound
In iron earth. All that disputed ground,
All those encumbered bodies, freeze
Into a blizzard of cold certainties:
'Perfect example of the art
Of war', 'a model chart

Judged so instructive that academies
All the world over trace
Again and yet again each move, each place . . .':
Decisive and meticulous strategies.
Meanwhile, among the stiffly rattling trees
Two thousand stones mark out
What it was all about.

Under the Campus

These squirrel-littered swards,
Brick groves of academe,
Have been here twelve decades.
Their towers cast a beam
For miles around, their trees
(Each labelled with its name)
All have their histories.

And yet an earlier claim
Lies underneath this trim
And pedagogic fame,
Primordial, alien, grim
Precursors of the place
Stowed in their shallow earth.
Their presence haunts the space

Two spade-lengths bring to birth:
Their distant life and death,
What they considered faith,
Their consecrated breath,
Remnants of clay and stone,
Ornament, weapon, bone,
Put out of mind and sight

Six centuries ago.
Under the towers' light,
Under the trees' brief glow,
A bead, a flint, a pot
Come humbly back, confront
Those who joined in the hunt,
And all these we forgot.

Philip Larkin in New Orleans

Suppose he had come here, two days after Mardi Gras,
The wrong time. It would be raining
In sheets up from the Delta, the banquettes awash
And the gutters running with all the festival trash:
Laughing-gas capsules, confetti, a tinsel star,
Cheap beads, purple and golden and green,
Bottle-caps, condoms, masks. Somewhere too far,
Somewhere too foreign. He would be complaining
This wasn't the dream he had had, the dream-place he'd been –
Tapping his feet in a bar in Bourbon or Basin, the moan
Of riverboats drifting through the Vieux Carré
Mingling with a familiar saxophone,
And the girls stepping out on the streets at the end of the day.

His Crescent City is much further off,
A paradise where love and trumpets play
In tune, and out of time, beyond belief
In ordinary days or usual grief,
A place in which all doubt is put away.
Tonight I caught his authentic other note,
Fixed, finite, steady in its monotone,
As I passed an old black with a graveyard cough,
An empty bottle, a funereal hat,
Who muttered something as he cleared his throat,
Trembled, and batted off the rain, and spat
Somewhere between Decatur and Wilk Row,
His hopes expelled with an enormous no.